What Would the American Founders Do?

Leadership Principles from the Federalist Papers

Henry T. Edmondson III, PhD

Cover © Shutterstock.com

www.kendallhunt.com
Send all inquiries to:
4050 Westmark Drive
Dubuque, IA 52004-1840

Contents

Introduction

From May 25 to September 17, 1787, delegates from the American colonies met together to fix the existing constitution, the Articles of Confederation, or to draft a new constitution for the country. The result was a new constitution. After the convention, however, their job was far from over: the citizens and politicians back home had to ratify the document, a difficult matter of salesmanship in several of the states. The opposition was formidable.

One state where the Constitution was hotly contested was New York. The fate of the Constitution was so precarious there that former Philadelphia delegate Alexander Hamilton invited two of his colleagues, John Jay of New York and Virginian James Madison, to join him in crafting a series of persuasive essays on behalf of the Constitution for the New York newspapers.

These 85 essays, written at the remarkable pace of 2 or 3 a week, were later collected in a volume called *The Federalist*; alternately they are called *The Federalist Papers*. Hamilton wrote about two-thirds of the papers, Madison about a third, and Jay only a handful. Following the custom of the day, they used a pseudonym drawn from Roman Republican history. Their choice was "Publius," a Roman consul who in the sixth century B.C. was instrumental in founding the Roman Republic and expelling the last Roman king. For some years, no one knew the authorship of the papers as the authors thought it best strategically to remain anonymous. Imagine such patience today when many political leaders race each other to the press or rush to sign multi-million deals for their memoirs!

The Federalist Papers were highly regarded in the decades following their publication. Late in life, President George Washington wrote to Hamilton explaining that the essays occupied "a most distinguished place in my library." Thomas Jefferson, who had nothing to do with writing the Constitution nor with writing the *Federalist Papers*, called them "the best commentary on the principles of government ... ever written." For the nineteenth-century English philosopher, John Stuart Mill, *The Federalist* was "the most instructive treatise we possess on federal government." The astute French political commentator, Alexis de Tocqueville, thought it "an excellent book, which ought to be familiar to the statesmen of all countries."

More recently, historians, jurists, and political scientists have generally agreed that *The Federalist* is the most important work of political philosophy and pragmatic government ever written in the United States. It has been compared to Plato's *Republic*, Aristotle's *Politics*, and Hobbes's *Leviathan*. In *Cohens v. Virginia* (1821), Chief Justice John Marshall wrote "It [*The Federalist*] is a complete commentary on our Constitution, and it is appealed to by all parties in the questions to which that instrument gave birth."

The Supreme Court has cited the papers in hundreds of cases and the authority of the papers seems to rise above political differences. The three justices who have cited the *Federalist Papers* the most are John Paul Stevens, Sandra Day O'Connor, and Antonin Scalia. The three of them have little more in common than their enthusiasm for the essays. Among the recent high-profile cases in which *The Federalist* has been invoked are *Gore v. Bush* (2000), which settled the debate over the 2000 presidential election, and *Printz v. New York* (1997), a landmark case dealing with handgun regulation.

The principles embedded in these essays are timeless, universal, and offer some of the best guidance one could hope for in public or private endeavors. Although *The Federalist* is first and foremost a work of political philosophy, leaders can profitably mine the essays for principles of leadership.

What, then, might be the particular advantages of studying leadership from *The Federalist*? There are several: First, those who wrote these essays were successful. They wrote a Constitution that is the oldest written Constitution in the world, and it has carried the country through a Civil War, two World Wars, the Vietnam War, wars in Afghanistan and Iraq, a spectacular terrorist attack in 2001, and several contested presidential elections, especially the election of 2000. It's not all been pretty, but the Constitution has endured.

It has been amended only 27 times, but those amendments have usually been momentous. Among other things, the amendments have

- *added the all-important Bill of Rights,*
- *clarified issues surrounding the Presidency (12th, 20th, 22nd, and 25th),*
- *freed slaves and guaranteed their voting rights and citizenship (13th, 14th, and 15th),*
- *guaranteed the right to vote to women (19th),*
- *guaranteed the right to vote to those 18 and older (26th),*
- *told Congressmen and Congresswomen that, if they gave themselves a raise, they couldn't enjoy it unless they were re-elected.*

This kind of success and durability should always get our attention. There are plenty of books on leadership written by people who have never really been tested in the crucible of leadership. Theory is nice but in matters like this, it needs to be tested by real life. Indeed, unlike some leadership studies, *The Federalist* is no exercise in idle speculation. America had no time for that; even after the miraculously successful War for Independence, the country was on the brink of collapse due to the failures of the Articles of Confederation. Though these essays deal with theoretical concepts, they simultaneously call for immediate and concrete action. The country, in 1787, was desperate for results.

That is not to say they were entirely successful. Many of the country's leaders, including those who owned slaves, wanted to abolish slavery as the Constitution was written but were unable to do so at that time. The choice seemed clear, at least at the moment: Demand the abolition of slavery and abandon any hope of uniting the country, or approve a constitution that everyone could agree on and wait until a later opportunity to rid the country of slavery. If the American Founders had pursued the former course and demanded an end to slavery in 1787, the country surely would have divided into at least two sections and the hope of ending slavery in the South would have faded from view. On the other hand, if slavery had been abolished in 1787, the country might have avoided a bloody civil war. At this point in time, it's difficult to know for certain what should have been done. We may never know.

The authors, moreover, were engaged in public life, rather than strictly private enterprises. The majority of books on leadership today arise from the private business sector and however valuable they may be, the public sector presents challenges not always shared by the private sector. At the same time the leadership principles embedded in *The Federalist* are universal and provide guidance for both sides of the public and private divide—and the non-profit sector. Anyone can benefit from them, whether they work for the State Department or Apple or the Red Cross.. Finally, the wisdom to be gained from *The Federalist* is not confined to the United States. Lessons on human nature, ambition, and the importance of history, for example, are relevant anytime, anywhere.

This book, then, has a double purpose: as advertised, it is a handbook for leaders or those aspiring to leadership—as well as those who are in a position to evaluate the leaders they follow. In addition, this is a modest, brief, but thoughtful introduction to the most important commentary on the U.S. Constitution ever produced in this country, *The Federalist Papers*.

1

Know When To Cut Your Losses

One of the hardest things to do is to cut your losses, that is, to recognize when an undertaking has failed irredeemably and should be abandoned. Publius argues for just such a strategy in Federalist Papers #15–22 when he maintains that the Articles of Confederation are beyond repair and must be discarded so that an entirely new and workable constitution can be written.

After a miraculous and successful War of Independence, the country was governed by the first so-called constitution, the Articles of Confederation, which only lasted 11 years, from 1777 to 1788.

Although the Articles kept the country together for over a decade, they turned into a disaster.

The Articles created a confederation out of the 13 colonies and like most confederations, the U.S. confederation failed, creating a crisis in the country as severe as the War for Independence, if not more so. After a remarkable triumph against Great Britain less than a decade earlier, the country was on the brink of collapse.

The government had no real power of taxation, no independent judiciary, no effective executive, no uniform system of currency, no power to regulate commercial transactions, no real ability to maintain and support an army, an incoherent foreign policy, and an unworkable amendment procedure.

Besides that, things were working just fine.

A revolt in Massachusetts called "Shay's Rebellion" demonstrated that anarchy loomed on the horizon. It was barely suppressed and every other state feared that the same could occur within their own borders.

George Washington admitted in correspondence to Henry Lee (Oct. 31, 1786) that the American experience was quickly demonstrating "that mankind when left to themselves are unfit for their own Government." He further lamented, "I am mortified beyond expression when I view the clouds that have spread over the brightest morn that ever dawned upon any Country."

The long winter of 1777–1778 at Valley Forge where soldiers of the Continental Army survived on inadequate rations and shivered in insufficient clothing was emblematic of the impotency of the government.

Serious discussions appeared in several prominent newspapers about the possibility of splitting the colonies into three separate countries: a southern republic, a middle republic, and a northeastern republic.

Even at that, one of the most difficult challenges facing Publius, the writer of the *Federalist* essays, was to convince the public and political leaders that the Articles of Confederation couldn't be saved. Failure had to be admitted.

And so Essays #15–22 are devoted to a discussion of why the Articles of Confederation won't work, or as Publius delicately puts it, "the insufficiency of the confederation to the union and thus to your political prosperity."

Although not all those in Philadelphia had actually signed the Articles of Confederation in 1777 (ratified in 1781), several men were at both events. Two of the most conspicuous were Gouvernour Morris and Roger Sherman. They had to admit to themselves and others that their earlier effort was failing. (No, it's not "Governor" Morris. Morris never was a governor. But he did have an interesting first name.)

But a fatal flaw in many leaders is the inability to admit failure and give up. They just don't know when to press "*Eject.*"

This seems to be a perennial problem in baseball's Minor Leagues so that, for some teams, counselors are available to help would-be major league players recognize that it's just not going to happen.

Knowing when to cut your losses, of course, means you can deal with failure. And the inability to do so is a problem for many.

Admitting your mistakes requires humility, but just as importantly, admitting your mistakes requires confidence, confidence in yourself and your ability.

This is to say, insecure men and women don't easily admit wrong. It is too devastating to their ego and sense of wellbeing. For that reason, insecurity is one of the most dangerous weaknesses in a leader. And it is important to recognize that insecurity takes on many forms, including aggressiveness and boasting.

Generally speaking, leaders should earn their position and responsibilities through experience and success; those who leapfrog into high positions may not bring enough confidence for the job.

When the going gets tough, the insecure just dig in. For the insecure, separating one's ego from the job at hand may be not only difficult but also impossible.

Leadership Principles:

- *Admit failure.*
- *Know when it is time to let go and change course.*
- *Learn to recognize insecurity in all its forms and be cautious about putting the insecure in leadership positions.*

2

Neither Men Nor Women Are Angels

Any successful leader must deal with human nature as he or she finds it. If not, managerial strategies and public policies may be doomed to failure since they begin with a faulty view of the way people think and behave. This is a principle feature of Publius's essays; namely, that a government, or any other enterprise for that matter, must be constructed on a sound view of human nature if it is to be successful.

Essay #51 contains several of the most memorable passages in *The Federalist*. In justifying a design for a government that builds upon man's gravitational pull toward self-interest, Publius rhetorically asks, "But what is government itself, but the greatest of all reflections on human nature?" He then explains, "If men were angels, no government would be necessary."

Indeed, Publius' view of human nature is one of the most conspicuous themes in *The Federalist*.

Stated differently, *The Federalist Papers* display a striking suspicion of human nature or at least a ready willingness to acknowledge how powerful a force self-interest may be.

The alternative rock group, The Shins, have a song entitled, "So Says I" that's all about human nature and government. In reference to Sir Thomas More's book *Utopia*, they sing, "Tell Thomas More we've had another failed attempt."

To be sure, Thomas More's *Utopia* is a lesson in what people are not like. That's why the tongue-in-cheek title means "no place."

Publius's opinion of human nature applies to all human endeavors. It's not a dark view, but it's realistic. For example, in Essay #6 he addresses the origins of war which include "the love of power," "the desire of pre-eminence and dominion," "the jealousy of power" as well as a variety of other "private passions."

In speaking of government design, Aristotle advised that the best government for a given time and place is "the best practicable" government. That is, not so much the absolutely best one, but the best one that will really work.

We have often heard the axiom: "The perfect is the enemy of the good." Publius, in response to his critics, explains in Paper #37 that "a faultless plan was not to be expected." In Paper #85 he reminds the reader, "Never expect to see a perfect work from imperfect man."

Publius is especially concerned about the behavior of men and women collectively. The Founders feared that no matter how good people are individually; when they become a group, the worst may emerge. Thus Publius feared the "mob" which could override the virtue of even the noblest citizen.

In an alarming observation, Publius famously explains in Paper #55, in a warning against making the House of Representatives too large, "Had every Athenian been a Socrates, Athens would still have been a mob." In other words, if every person in Athens had been as good a person as Socrates, when those people got together, they may still have become a lawless, misbehaving mob.

The New York Herald noted in 1864 that one of the keys to Abraham Lincoln's success was his "shrewd perception of the ins and outs of poor, weak human nature" which has enabled him to master difficulties that would have swamped any other man." Biographer Richard Brookhiser quotes George Washington "We must take the passions of men as nature has given them."

Brookhiser elaborates, "People can be warned or persuaded or inspired. They can be led. That goes for anyone you meet; that goes for yourself. Take a good look at people as they are and then take them someplace else. A leader must know who he is, and who he is dealing with; and then he must lead."

How does this translate into ordinary day-to-day leadership?

Organizational theorist Chester Barnard, who also served as the CEO of New Jersey Bell Telephone, was way ahead of his time with his 1938 book *Functions of the Executive*. He taught, contrary to the top-down theories of the time, and the prevalent ideas of what was called scientific management, that efficiency and effectiveness come from discerning the motives and incentives of the employee and, to the extent possible, satisfying those individual interests. That is, managing with a clear view of the interests of the employee as well as the interests of the organization and its leadership.

The same considerations apply to making public policy: The late Senator Daniel Patrick Moynihan once observed that he had attended hundreds of meetings where people discussed the ways stock markets behave, but he had not once in his long career attended a meeting where the behavior of people was discussed. But the way people behave is the first principle of government. Despite billions of dollars being invested in America's social policy in the 1960s by means of the Great Society programs, there is some evidence that poverty did not improve. In fact, it may be that the condition of the underclass became worse because some of the programs rested on flawed views of what people are like and how they behave.

Put in everyday terms, a successful leader is a good judge of character, both of people in particular and people in general. He or she is not naive, nor shocked when people behave in self-interested ways and do not respond to calls for the "common good."

Likewise the leader is not shocked when people "rise above themselves" and act in noble ways. The good leader understands that people are complex and sometimes self-contradictory.

The successful leader takes human nature as it is, not as she or he wishes it might be. The leader is neither naive nor cynical.

LEADERSHIP PRINCIPLES:

- *Realize that people, for all their good qualities, are predictably self-interested. In fact, self-interest may not necessarily be a vice. Lead accordingly.*
- *Be realistic about human nature in leading and making decisions and setting policy.*
- *Take people as they are: encourage and praise what is good, make appropriate accommodations for what is not.*

3

Is "Post-Partisanship" Possible?

One of the most conspicuous features of Publius's "new science of politics," as he puts it, is the idea that factions united by narrow self-interest simply can't be avoided because such tendencies are "sown in the nature of man." What does this imply then, for leadership? Publius argues for an institutional arrangement that not only accepts factions, but also takes advantage of them. Accordingly, one of the principles of leadership is the ability of the leader to manage conflict in positive ways.

If men and women consistently act in self-interested ways, what kind of challenge does this present for managing groups? We've sometimes heard the promise of a post-partisan era or some sort of new world order in which we overcome all our antagonisms and work together in civic and global harmony.

We're still waiting. But in the meantime, there are conflicts to be dealt with.

In Federalist Paper #10, Publius argues that factions are "sown in the nature of man." This is the self-interest discussed in the previous section as it plays out in competing groups. In other ways, if people are self-interested, so are groups. By "factions" Publius means self-regarding groups that may be willing to violate the rights of others.

But Publius warns that we can eliminate aggressively self-interested partisanship only by changing man's nature or by denying him liberty. One cure rests on a fantasy; the other is worse than the disease. In other words, in a democracy, we will always have self-promoting groups.

In Essay #1, Publius argues that an impartial disinterested debate over the Constitution is "more ardently to be wished for, than seriously to be expected." The constitutional "plan," he explains, "affects too many particular interests." Though in some cases, disagreement may come from "honest errors," more likely is the problem of political "greed, self-aggrandizement" and "party opposition."

So, if people behave in a disinterested way, count yourself lucky. It doesn't always happen.

In Essay #37, Publius notes how hard it is for people to even discuss serious matters in a straightforward manner. Such discussions tend to go to extremes. He writes, "It is a misfortune, inseparable from human affairs, that public measures are rarely investigated with that spirit of moderation which is essential to a just estimate of . . . the public good."

He could have been talking about last week. Or the week before.

He further notes that the Constitutional Convention seemed to have enjoyed a rare fleeting moment in which some elements of factionalism were sidestepped, but that experience was the exception that proves the rule.

Publius also explains, however, that partisanship can be used constructively. Part of his strategy is entailed in the size of the country itself: if you have enough competing factions, none will be able to gain the upper hand. In other words, far from trying to get everyone to "get along," let a thousand arguments bloom, and in that fertile, floral field, stability and security are to be found.

This was a radical idea in Philadelphia in 1787, but it is one of the principal political doctrines that won the day. It was also the argument that justified trying to establish a republic in such a large country as ours: the more space, the more factions.

The first implication of this is that contemporary leaders must be prepared for conflict and learn to manage it—to the degree possible—in a constructive fashion.

In far too many groups—whether they be a business group, a political group, or a religious group—leaders may pursue a short cut to a kind of "paper unity." It looks pretty on the outside, but inside is ugly disagreement and unstable dissatisfaction. If the problems aren't really addressed, they will fester as apathy or resentment.

So the leader must not be afraid of conflict; rather, he or she must learn to manage it. Admittedly this is both a skill and an inherent talent—it can't easily be learned from a management textbook—but it is essential for a great organization.

Managing conflict, moreover, is not simply a reactionary strategy; in many cases, it's best to take charge and draw out disagreements before they rear their head in more difficult ways.

Actively draw out disagreements where they already exist. But this may take creativity and determination on the part of the leader.

Anonymous surveys may not be enough. Neither may it be sufficient to simply offer, "My door is always open," because people too often consider candor to be risky.

"Speak freely," a phrase borrowed from the military, is one of the skills we most need for good leadership. However, this is hard to do if the group is too large—better in smaller groups. Otherwise there are two problems: the leader gets defensive despite her best efforts not to, or the subordinates feel patronized because the leader can only give token responses at best.

LEADERSHIP PRINCIPLES:

- *Don't be surprised to find conflict and factions. Learn to use them constructively and imaginatively.*
- *Seek candid input from those around you, even if you must be creative to get it.*
- *Don't surround yourself with "yes men" or "yes woman." As someone once remarked, "Good leaders don't take 'yes' for an answer."*
- *If conducted tactfully, sometimes competition among groups in an organization can be productive—and fun!*

4

It's Not "Just Rhetoric"

Many an effective leader has fallen short because he or she is a poor com-municator. A stirring vision, great ideas, and meaningful objectives may all fall stillborn if the leader can't communicate. Leaders today could use a page from The Federalist *because Publius is a master at getting the point across.*

"Rhetoric" has become a dirty word. People use it to mean insincere, manipulative speech. "You can't believe what he says—it's just rhetoric!" "Don't listen to her: it's just a bunch of empty rhetoric!"

But rhetoric, properly understood, enjoys a noble heritage. One of Aristotle's most accessible and practical books is simply entitled *The Rhetoric*. It is a manual of sorts on how to understand your audience and how to get your message across without sacrificing your integrity. Rhetoric was once part of the ancient "trivium" (grammar, logic, and rhetoric) in schools and even now, rhetoric is enjoying a comeback as a college discipline, though admittedly with some changes.

Among other things, Aristotle argues that the personal character of a speaker always has a way of peeping out around the edges. Accordingly, Aristotle argues that the speaker's character, or "ethos," is critical to effective communication.

Publius is a master of rhetoric.

When we first begin reading the Federalist Papers, I offer my students a little PowerPoint rubric I call "How To Read the Federalist Papers."

Briefly, it consists of the following steps:

- *Identify the theme of the essay.*

- *Locate the paper in the overall organization of The Federalist, especially if it is part of a series, such as papers #47–51 on Separation of Powers, #52–61 on the House, #62–66 on the Senate, #67–77 on the Presidency, and #78–83 on the Judiciary.*

- *Identify the objection the essay is written to refute. In other words, the Federalist essays are not written in a vacuum; rather, every paper is written to meet criticism of the newly proposed Constitution and if you don't know the objection, you can't fully understand the argument.*

- *Identify the logic of the paper and the way in which it is organized: for the papers on the Presidency, the primary argument is for a president at least as strong as the one proposed in the Constitution; the argument of Papers #67–#77, then, outlines the features of a strong chief executive. Publius's logic is generally pretty effective, and he knows how to expose the illogic of his opponent.*

In summary, the Federalist essays are well constructed and persuasively argued. But Publius knew how to apply different tactics to different situations.

In paper #81 on the Judiciary, Publius accuses his opponents of "false reasoning" proceeding from "misconceived fact." This is just one of the many examples in which Publius shrewdly sets his opponents back on the defensive.

Publius, however, also knows when to pay respect to his opponent's argument. In Papers #47–51, he concedes the importance of the Anti-Federalist concerns that the new Constitution does not adhere to the principle of separation of powers. He disagrees, but he begins from a position of respect.

On the other hand, he knows when the argument of his opponents does not deserve respect. In Paper #38, he uses a powerful metaphor: He compares the opponents of the Constitution to those who would oppose critical medical treatment for a dying patient but are unable to offer an alternative.

In Paper #67, Publius's rhetoric turns angry—a rare instance, to be sure— as he argues that the Anti-Federalists have willfully distorted the design for the Chief Executive.

In order to appreciate the power of great oratory we need to look no farther than the brilliance of Martin Luther King, Jr.'s rhetoric. He is one of the most eloquent orators this country has ever produced.

One of the keys to King's success was his use of imagery, of the use of the metaphor.

Winston Churchill's biographer argues as well that the prime minister's oratorical success rested in part on his ability to create word pictures.

When his fellow parliamentarians were unable to respond in a decisive fashion to the Nazi threat, Churchill called them "boneless wonders," in reference to a local circus freak, called "The Boneless Wonder," who was afflicted with a severely underdeveloped skeletal system.

For the day-to-day leader, however, rhetorical genius is not necessary. Everyone has their own style, and in many cases, the plain and ordinary speech will do just fine. Don't try to be something you are not. If you are not a joke-teller, then preserve your dignity and don't try to tell jokes. But do be clear and organized and concise. No one appreciates your wasting their time with disorganized, rambling, and unfocused speech. And please, please, don't try to give an answer before you understand the question! Nor should you give an answer to a question that *wasn't asked* instead of answering *what is asked*.

<h3 style="text-align:center; color:#3333aa;">LEADERSHIP PRINCIPLES:</h3>

- *Communication is as much a matter of who you are as what you say.*
- *Understand the mood of your audience. Are they excited? Inspired? Disappointed? Angry? Adjust your communication accordingly.*
- *Give credit to different opinions when credit is due; if it is not, don't patronize.*
- *Draw word pictures when you can. You don't have to be an artist to do so.*
- *Follow your own style—don't try to be something you are not. People always appreciate simple, clear, organized, and sincere speech.*

5

Integrity Is Indispensable

The Federalist Papers are well known for their emphasis on institutions, processes, and the usefulness of self-interest, rather than an appeal to personal virtue as the safeguard of government. That said, it is also true that an expectation for civic virtue in leaders and citizens alike underlies these essays. This is not only an abstract hope—many of the Founders themselves were models of integrity, even if they were flawed human beings.

This principle may come as a surprise for those familiar with the *Federalist Papers,* and familiar with the debates over how much our Constitutional system relies on— or does not rely upon—virtuous people.

To be sure, the Constitution is designed so that people of no more than mediocre talent and character could be at the helm and the ship would not sink.

Someone once remarked that there have been only a handful of times when "the pot was boiling over," that is, when we were super-saturated with men and women of talent. One time was the era of the Greek philosophers; another time was the American Founding.

Thomas Jefferson thought the Constitutional Convention was an assembly of "demi-gods," so great was the collection of intelligence and character.

This is not to say that the American Founders were perfect—far from it. But they were nonetheless men of character, surrounded by women of character. Though the women get second billing, they formed part of the backbone of the integrity of the nation.

For example, the late NPR correspondent Cokie Roberts celebrates several of these women in her popular book, *Founding Mothers,* which features chapters on Abigail Adams, Martha Washington, and sixteen-year-old Eliza Lucas Pickney, who ran a South Carolina plantation by day and read Plutarch and Virgil by night. In addition, she introduced indigo to American agriculture, which became a component of the colonial economy.

Not to be forgotten are the courageous black men and women of sterling character who have done so much to shape the nation. They include Frederick Douglass, Harriett Tubman, Fannie Lou Hammer, W.E.B. Dubois, Sojourner Truth, Rosa Parks, James Farmer, John Lewis, Roy Wilkins, Martin Luther King, Jr., Medgar Evers—the list goes on.

But the pot doesn't boil over very often. Sometimes it doesn't even produce a simmer.

Nonetheless, although Publius doesn't talk much about the virtuous leader—since he can't be sure we will always have them in the future—he does acknowledge how crucial virtue is.

In Paper #55, Publius observes that though we must keep in mind our weakness of character, at the same time we need to encourage and rely upon our character strengths. He writes that just as "there is a degree of depravity in mankind, which requires a certain degree of circumspection and distrust: so there are other qualities in human nature, which justify a certain portion of esteem and confidence." Just as people can give in to their bad qualities, Publius assures us that we can have a certain amount of confidence that we can encourage their good qualities as well.

In fact, in a democracy, we really need these qualities because if are engaged in self-government, we need people to be as virtuous as possible because, as he says, "Republican government presupposes the existence of these qualities in a HIGHER degree than any other form."

In other words, despite man's lower tendencies, he nonetheless has the capacity for a life of virtue, and republican government needs that virtue more than any other form of government—both from the leaders and the citizens.

Simply put, self-government requires self-governing people. Self-governing people are people of integrity.

One of Publius' arguments for the life tenure of justices to the Supreme Court is that it is more likely to attract and retain men and women of integrity. In Paper #78, Publius argues that a limited term of office for justices might be less likely to encourage the kind of "fit characters" who are so necessary to impartial adjudication. That's one of the reasons why justices are appointed for life.

It is no surprise then how preoccupied many of the Founders were with moral and civic education, about which they corresponded and wrote constantly. Such discussions are found in the writings of Thomas Jefferson, George Washington, and Benjamin Rush, to name only the most prominent.

The country got lucky because it had a man of integrity at the helm, George Washington, who was instrumental not only in the successful prosecution of the Revolutionary War, but also in the success of the first two presidential administrations. In addition, though he said little, Washington's presence alone at the Constitutional Convention kept every delegate on his best behavior.

Joseph Addison's (1672–1719) play "Cato: A Tragedy," first staged in 1713, inspired many enlightened thinkers in the eighteenth century. It is a portrayal of the Roman senator Cato the Younger (95–46 B.C.E.) who was willing to take his own life rather than to live under the tyrannical rule of Julius Caesar.

George Washington remarked it was his favorite play and he had it performed for his men in Valley Forge during the revolution as a source of inspiration in desperate times. Washington found in the play a powerful statement on patriotism, liberty, virtue, and honor. He quoted from it extensively in his writings.

Nathan Hale echoed another line from the play, right before he was hanged by the British as a spy: "I regret, but that I have only one life to give to my country."

One of the most important character traits for a leader is magnanimity; a virtue celebrated by Aristotle and revered by the Founding Generation. It literally means having a "great soul." It is the opposite of pettiness. Not only does the magnanimous leader not engage in purposeless criticism or gossip, neither does the leader retaliate if he or she is the subject of such abuse.

Winston Churchill's biographer Steven Hayward explains, "The most remarkable example of Churchill's magnanimity was his refusal to criticize the British people when they voted him out of office in a landslide just two months after the war ended in 1945. When a colleague spoke to Churchill of the "ingratitude" of the people as the votes were coming in on election night, Churchill replied: "Oh no, I wouldn't call it that. They have had a very hard time."

After Washington's death Jefferson responds to a correspondent at length about Washington's character, especially his habit of prudence. At the same time, he doesn't play down Washington's rare but spectacular fits of anger.

Prudence also goes by the name "practical wisdom" which means you not only understand moral principles, but you also know how they should be applied day-to-day.

But these are mostly high-profile illustrations of integrity. In their book *Exemplary Public Administrators*, Terry Anderson and Dale Wright note the everyday integrity on display at all levels of public life, highlighting, for example, the uncompromising character of George Hartzog of the National Parks Service; the late Beverlee Myers who fought to maintain her integrity in the bureaucracy of U.S. health care administration first in D.C.; and Surgeon General C. Everett Koop who, while strict in his evangelical Christian views, nonetheless forced himself to draw a distinction between his personal ideals on the one hand, and, on the other hand, public policies on AIDS and abortion that he deemed appropriate for the public at large.

One of the best stories of character appears in the autobiography of Frederick Douglass. Douglass was an escaped slave who taught himself to read and eventually became a friend of Abraham Lincoln and served in his administration. Before his escape, Douglass had proved himself to be such a recalcitrant slave that he was sent to Stephen Covey, a notorious slave-breaker.

Covey was almost successful until one sweltering afternoon Douglass rebelled against the physical, emotional, and psychological abuse and fought Covey to a draw in a fistfight. Covey never attempted to break Douglass again. At that point, Douglass realized that his character could never be broken because, as he put it, "I decided I wasn't afraid to die."

Now *that* is character.

LEADERSHIP PRINCIPLES:

- *While an organization may not be solely dependent on men and women of character, in the long run, they are indispensable to its success. An acceptance of self-interest does not mean that integrity is not important.*
- *Certain character traits are particular to leadership, especially magnanimity and prudence. Look for it and cultivate it.*
- *Character is not gender-specific: you are as likely to find it in women as men; in fact, some traits of character may be more readily found in women.*

6

Ambition Comes With the Territory

Most great writers on leadership agree on this fundamental point: if you want good leadership, you must be prepared for the ambition that comes with it. Robust ambition, good leader; feeble ambition, poor leader. Understanding that, the question then becomes: how do you manage that ambition while enjoying strong leadership?

One of the most memorable lines of *The Federalist* comes from #51. In the construction of the institutions of government, Publius argues that "ambition must be made to counteract ambition." In other words, leaders of ambition can't and shouldn't be discouraged. Rather, you must keep such ambitious people in check with more ambitious people. Strong leaders need strong leaders.

To be sure, ambition is one of the most common human traits.

Michael Leden in his book *Machiavelli on Modern Leadership* argues that "human ambition is unlimited, that of both individuals and the institutions they create." He further argues that the "fight for ambition . . . is so powerful in human breasts that no matter to what rank they rise it never abandons them."

Ambition is a given; it can't be eliminated. Nor should it, not if you want strong leaders.

Legendary General George Patton was critical to the Allied effort in North Africa, Sicily, and the European Theater of Operations. His was a complex personality, but this much is clear: he was ambitious from an early age. A visitor to West Point today can look at Patton's class notebooks when the future general was only a cadet. From time to time in the margins of those notebooks, the 18-year-old Patton wrote instructions to his future biographers.

Both Alexander Hamilton and the French officer who joined the cause of the American Revolution, the Marquis de Lafayette, were explicit about their private motives for military service. As Lafayette put it: I am seeking glory. And the colonies were glad he was.

We tend, however, to condemn ambition too quickly. To call someone "ambitious" is often a criticism, not a compliment. Alex de Tocqueville explained the difference between "low" and "high" ambition: Low ambition is entirely self-centered; high ambition still seeks personal fame but in the service of the public good.

Ambition, according to Aristotle, is a passion. It can be used for good or bad. Thus the leader has two challenges: managing his own ambition and the ambition of others.

Federalist #72 addresses what Publius approvingly calls "the love of fame, the ruling passion of the noblest minds, which would prompt a man to plan and undertake extensive and arduous enterprises for the public benefit." In the same essay, Publius notes that those with such a ruling passion will not be content to simply tend the garden that their predecessor has planted; each president will want to establish his own "legacy."

A young Abraham Lincoln describes such ruling passion a half-century later in his precocious "Young Man's Lyceum Speech," where he warns of the passing of the Founding Generation and the need to control the next generation of leaders. These leaders will be, as he puts it, of "the family of the lion, the tribe of the eagle."

For Publius, such ambition is not limited to the executive office. In paper #57, Publius describes the elements that will tie the members of the House of Representative to his constituents: "Duty, gratitude, interest, [and] ambition itself."

Historian Don E. Fehrenbacher describes "Lincolns profound and elevated sense of ambition—an ambition notably free of pettiness, malice and overindulgences." Fehrenbacher continues, "Though Lincoln desired success as fiercely as any of his rivals, he did not allow his quest for office to consume the kindness and open-heartedness with which he treated supporters and rivals alike, nor alter his steady commitment to the antislavery cause."

Lincoln also had the ambition of others to manage.

In *Team of Rivals*, Doris Kearns Goodwin explores Lincoln's political genius by examining his relationships with three men he selected for his cabinet, all of whom were his opponents for the Republican nomination in 1860: William H. Seward, Salmon P. Chase, and Edward Bates.

These men, all accomplished, dignified, and nationally known, originally disdained Lincoln for his backwoods upbringing and lack of experience. They were shocked and humiliated at losing to this relatively obscure Illinois lawyer with calloused hands.

Yet Lincoln not only convinced them to join his administration—Seward as secretary of state, Chase as secretary of the treasury, and Bates as attorney general—he ultimately gained their admiration and respect as well.

How he soothed egos, turned rivals into allies, and dealt with many challenges to his leadership, all for the sake of the greater good, are largely what Goodwin's book is about. Had he not possessed the wisdom and confidence to select and work with the best people, she argues, he could not have led the nation through one of its darkest periods.

Salmon Chase was as difficult as he was capable. Pennsylvania editor Alexander K. McClure wrote "Salmon P. Chase was the most irritating fly in the Lincoln ointment from the inauguration of the new administration in 1861 until the 29th of June, 1864, when his resignation as Secretary of the Treasury was finally accepted. He was an annual "resigner" in the Cabinet, having petulantly tendered his resignation in 1862, again in 1863, and again in 1864, when he was probably surprised by Mr. Lincoln's acceptance of it."

Fellow Ohioan Benjamin Wade once said: "Chase is a good man, but his theology is unsound. He thinks there is a fourth person in the Holy Trinity."

LEADERSHIP PRINCIPLES:

- *Ambition is not intrinsically bad; on the contrary, it is part and parcel of strong leadership.*
- *Learn to manage ambition in the leaders around you even if it means knowing how to deal with big egos—which it might.*
- *Learn to understand your own ambition: is it "bad" or "good"? Is it only for yourself or is it also in the interest of the common good?*

7

Know Your History

What made the arguments for the new Constitution so strong, both at the Philadelphia Convention and in the ensuing ratification debates, was, in part, the Federalists' command of history. What does this mean for the leader today? It means two things: one, today's leader should appreciate institutional memory, the history of the organization of which he is a part. Secondly, "know your history" means the same thing for today's leader that it did for the American Founders: the more history you know, the better equipped you are to deal with the present and to prepare for the future.

Reading through the *Federalist Papers*, we see that Publius compared the American endeavor in one way or the other with a multitude of historical entities and endeavors and drew lessons from those historical examples. Here is but a sample of Publius' vast historical knowledge as displayed in these essays. It is, at the same time, mind-numbing and impressive.

- **The Achaean League** *(fifth century B.C. to 150 B.C.), one of the most successful federated republics in history, a stronghold of freedom in Greece*
- **The Aetolian League**, *which was modeled after Achaean League*
- **Alexander the Great's empires** *and his attempts to leave workable governments in his various conquered territories*
- **The Amphictyonic Council,** *a loose confederation of ancient Greek city-states dating back to early Greek history.*
- **The Kingdom of Aragon** *in northeastern Spain*
- **The Aulic Council,** *intended as the chief administrative arm of the Holy Roman Emperor*

Why were the American Founders successful? Their knowledge of the history of republics and democracy was encyclopedic. They were determined not to commit the errors of the past but to learn from them.

Too often, though, ventures and projects fail because those who manage them act as if this is the first time it has ever been tried.

Moshe Dayan, the Israeli military leader and politician who was instrumental in Israel's stunning victory in the Six-Day War in 1967, would at times read accounts of the ancient Old Testament battles and then visit the sites where the battles occurred to see what he might learn about successful strategy.

All leaders—and young leaders especially—have an obligation to learn from history and to draw upon the experience of others.

History and experience, moreover, are safeguards against the danger of abstract theory.

In Federalist Paper #6, Publius provides a damning indictment of grand but untested schemes. He could be speaking yesterday when he asks,

"Have we not already seen enough of the fallacy and extravagance of those idle theories which have amused us with promises of an exemption from the imperfections, the weaknesses, and the evils incident to society in every shape?"

For Publius, history is prevention against utopian dreams and against the complaints that the Philadelphia Constitution was not perfect. He again asks in Paper #6, if it isn't time to recognize there will never be a "golden age" of "perfect wisdom and perfect virtue."

On an everyday level, we are not talking about the need for a PhD in history. Sometimes it is just a matter of learning from experience.

Experience, in turn, brings prudence, the practical wisdom needed to know to take general concepts and apply them to specific situations.

An inescapable corollary to this is that when young men and women assume leadership, they have a special challenge: they are short on experience. That's why Aristotle, in his *Politics*, warned that you might find a good youthful theoretical mathematician, but a young man of prudence is hard to find.

For that reason, mentorships are often valuable practices in raising strong leaders, an idea that comes from the relationship that Odysseus son Telemachus had with Odysseus' old friend, Mentor, while awaiting his father's return.

On the ground level, this also may translate into an obligation to maintain the institutional memory of a given organization.

I once had the privilege of teaching a course on Leadership and Ethics aboard one of the U.S.'s "super aircraft carriers." At that time the leadership of the ship was superb. However, shortly thereafter a change of command occurred and the incoming commanding officer, a former F/A-18 pilot, was given a tour of the ship. One of the officers privately expressed his dismay that the new CO seemed uninterested in the managerial and organizational history of the vessel. I was not surprised, then, when several years later I heard that morale among the crew of 5000 sailors and pilots had noticeably dipped during the new CO's tenure.

LEADERSHIP PRINCIPLES:

- *Be a student of history. If you don't care for straight history itself, enjoy historical novels, and cinema that deals with history in dramatic fashion. Attend historical memorials and reenactments.*
- *Learn from experience.*
- *If you are new to an organization, make an effort to explore its institutional memory.*
- *Whatever your profession, look for a mentor as may be appropriate in your line of work.*
- *Avoid people who act as if the world was created yesterday (by them)*

Don't Avoid Compromising Situations

The Constitution has been called a "bundle of compromises" and indeed, it involved several "deals" that were struck between those who disagreed on fundamental issues. These include compromises over the role of government, compromises over slavery, compromises over representation in the national government, compromises over the balance of power between the national government and the state governments, and difficulty agreements over the design of the chief executive. Generally speaking, success in leadership is more often achieved by a series of compromises rather than absolute victories.

Many are familiar with the balance that was achieved between the Virginia Plan and the New Jersey Plan by means of the Connecticut Compromise. The contest balance is often referred to as the Big State Plan versus the Small State even if that is an over-simplification. Whatever you call it, it was not an easy negotiation.

The present design of the president is also the result of a great deal of negotiating. The office is not as constitutionally strong as James Madison or Alexander Hamilton wanted; nor is it the relatively weak executive council that others proposed.

One of the problems with compromise is that no one may be happy. For that reason, settling on an agreement may take more courage than assuming an aggressive and unyielding posture. Compromises may look ugly, and they can be misrepresented or misunderstood.

There were several compromises over slavery in the Constitution. To properly understand them, it is important to note how deeply some of the principal Founders opposed slavery—even if they found themselves in a traditional slave-owning family. It is also important to note that for many, simply freeing slaves might not have been easy because freed slaves had to receive financial support from their former owners. Furthermore, because of country-wide racial prejudice, in the North as well as the South, freedmen might find that emancipation placed them in an environment more dangerous than that of their previous bondage.

Even if leaders of the Founding Generation might have been perplexed at the best way to dismantle the institution of slavery, they often held principled opposition to the institution. Here are several telling quotes:

- *"There is not a man living who wishes more sincerely than I do, to see a plan adopted for the abolition of [slavery]"* —George Washington
- *"Every measure of prudence, therefore, ought to be assumed for the eventual total extirpation of slavery from the United States . . . I have, through my whole life, held the practice of slavery in . . . abhorrence"* —John Adams
- *"We have seen the mere distinction of color made in the most enlightened period of time, a ground of the most oppressive dominion ever exercised by man over man."* —James Madison

Compromises are often misunderstood and the one making the compromise may be criticized by those on both sides of the deal. Such has been the case with the infamous "3/5 Compromise" in Article I, Section 2 of the Constitution by which slaves were counted as 3/5 for purposes of representation and taxation. This has been criticized because, it is alleged, it treats a black man as 2/5 less than a human being. But that is a superficial and erroneous criticism. First of all, if slaves had been counted equivalent to non-slaves, because of the number of slaves, the southern states would have had greater representation in the House of Representatives, and accordingly more political power. Even counting slaves 3/5 rather than 5/5 gave the slave-owning states additional political weight.

Nonetheless every five enslaved individuals only counted as three people for purposes of representation—not what the South wanted at the time.

In Federalist Paper #54, moreover, Publius takes the opportunity to point out that the compromise forced slave-owners to recognize that slaves were not just property but human beings as well. In other words, if slave-owning states wanted slaves to count toward representation in Congress, they couldn't be merely property because no other property is calculated into the number of representatives the state might have. Representation in Congress is not determined by horses or wagons. Only human beings count.

Publius even twists the knife by using language that puts slavery in the worst possible light. The slave is "compelled to labor," he is "vendible," that he is up for sale from one master to another. He is "degraded from the human rank," and he is "classified with the irrational animals."

So, given that the Federalist Papers grew in popularity after the Constitution was ratified, certain slave-owners may have thought in the years to come that they may have had lost as much or more than they gained in the 3/5 Compromise.

More generally, even though compromises are unavoidable, the insightful leader may be able to gain more than meets the eye. But she must be prepared for the criticism of those who are not so insightful; or, worse, those who attack the leader for personal gain.

LEADERSHIP PRINCIPLES:

- *Know when and how to compromise.*
- *Remember that compromises may not be understood, especially by those who want to criticize the compromise for their own advantage.*
- *Remember as well that compromises may not be popular, even if they are the right thing to do or at least the best possible in the situation.*
- *Finally, remember that a compromise may be more of a victory than many realize.*

9

Imagine That! Leaders Need Vision

Some leadership skills can be taught, some cannot. Among the latter category is the ability a true leader must have to see what others can't see, to have vision. Closely related is the quality of imagination, the ability to think creatively, to think outside of the box. Cultivating such qualities may be the most elusive quest of all.

Vision is a recurrent theme in leadership studies. Leaders must see beyond the present. They must be able to articulate their vision. And they must be able to persuade others to adopt that vision.

What is the difference between management and leadership? Among other things, leaders are expected to see the big picture, to articulate expansive ideas, to think outside of the box, to get to the heart of the matter. Managers, for the most part, work *inside* the box. Their task is to take what is in front of them and ensure it works well.

The argument over the new American government was won largely in the arena of ideas. Rhetorical strategy and tactics were important, but even more critical was the battle over the principles of government, power, and human nature.

Publius was a visionary. Conservatives today like to claim Publius as their own, but they should take note that he wasn't always conservative; in some ways he was downright radical. After all, he advocated entirely discarding one government and replacing it with another unproven system of government.

He first of all, and most importantly, had to argue that the real danger to the country was not from a strong government, but from a weak government, a government that would be incapable of containing man's gravitational pull toward anarchy.

He further introduced the innovative idea that factions, however pernicious they might be, could be used constructively as a means of achieving an uneasy, but workable, stability.

He explained, perhaps more clearly than any other political theorist, that ambition is here to stay, and like factions, ambition could only be balanced with more, not less, ambition.

He argued, in Papers 67–77, that, despite the abuse the colonies had suffered under King George III, the country should once again adopt a strong executive.

Not an easy sell.

Another idea he emphasized is this: Don't ask the government to do what you don't give it the power to do. Means must always be proportionate to ends, Publius argued.

He applied that logic across the board. Although he introduces the idea as early as Essay #37, he reiterates the principle in a discussion of the Judiciary in Paper #80. And however much the Anti-Federalists might have disliked this principle, it was irrefutable.

Publius is always one step ahead of his opponents, to the extent that the Anti-Federalists were branded as the reactionaries.

At the same time, Publius does not paint himself into a corner. In several places he explains that the business of building a government involves a great deal of imprecision, and for that reason, he also says in Paper #37 that we must allow room for what he calls the "liquidation" of the meaning of the Constitution; that is, some of its meaning and application will unfold over time.

Both Federalist Paper #1 and the last paper, #85, stand as bookends to the series and they are both visionary essays. They help the reader see America's moment in history, and both papers warn of the catastrophe that will ensue if the country doesn't get it right.

At stake, Publius argues in #1, is nothing less than "the existence of the UNION." He concludes in #85, with a disturbing picture "A NATION without a NATIONAL GOVERNMENT, is an awful spectacle."

Good leaders don't have to be philosophers. But they do need imagination, creativity, vision, and the ability to grasp the big picture—to understand the principles at work in a given environment.

It is no surprise then that many corporations are finding that liberal arts graduates make the best leaders. Without such an education, graduates may be narrow-minded, lacking the imagination needed for demanding leadership.

10

Keep the Faith

Seeking the inspiration, guidance, and protection of something greater and higher than ourselves never falls out of fashion. One of the interesting themes in The Federalist *is the occasional acknowledgment that something stands behind the human endeavor. The best leaders seem to know this and are not afraid to say so.*

We live in a world that too often gives in to the urge to cleanse society of any practice, or any memory, of something bigger and better than ourselves.

Such was not the case with Publius. Although the Constitution makes no explicit sectarian reference to God, the Federalist Papers are richly colored with the idea that Providence has been, and should be, involved with American destiny.

In Essay #2, Publius suggests a "Design of Providence" in the formative stages of America.

In Essay #37, Publius says that no honest person can look on what has happened in the formation of America and not believe that something greater than ourselves has been at work. He writes, "It is impossible for any man of candor to reflect on this circumstance, without partaking of the astonishment. It is impossible for the man of pious reflection, not to perceive in it a finger of the Almighty Hand, which has been so frequently and signally extended to our relief in the critical stages of the revolution."

In Nicholas Wade's book, *The Faith Instinct,* the author suggests that an inclination toward something beyond us is in our genes. We can only deny it with effort or forced apathy.

Some might call piety out of fashion. Even so, contemporary leaders of all persuasions seem incapable of resisting the temptation to invoke God's blessings in public addresses. Leaders frequently offer "thoughts and prayers" for the unfortunate victims of natural disasters. Participants at endless Middle East summits, for example, are invariably the recipients of such prayers. Contemporary practice suggests that an attitude of piety that is based on humility is always in fashion. No situation, moreover, seems as likely to induce piety as war, distress, or disaster.

On July 29, 1967, the Super Carrier USS Foresttal suffered an unimaginable disaster that permanently changed both the construction of and training for U.S. Navy aircraft carriers. While stationed off the coast of North Vietnam, an electric generator used to start jet engines sent a wayward electrical impulse to an F-4B Phantom jet on the flight deck of the carrier. The impulse caused a missile to fire across the deck hitting another aircraft that in turn ignited a jet fuel explosion followed by an uncontrollable raging fire. By the end of the day, the carrier had suffered nine major on-board detonations of the ship's own 500- and 1,000-pound armaments, and countless smaller missile explosions, including shrapnel-filled anti-radar ordinances.

The ensuing holocaust claimed 134 lives, including scores of sailors who were instantaneously cremated in below-deck sections of the ship while sleeping in their bunks. Many more were maimed or lost their lives to fire and explosions while heroically fighting to control the inferno that threatened the entire *Forrestal* crew of 5000 and even nearby ships of the *Forrestal* battle group.

When the conflagration was finally contained, Commanding Officer Captain John K. Beeling, in perhaps the most challenging duty of his career, addressed the physically exhausted and emotionally shattered survivors, many of whom had spent hours collecting the charred remains and fragments of their fellow sailors.

What does a leader say at such a time? What words can acknowledge the ship's immeasurable tragedy and assuage the crew's unspeakable grief, yet at the same time, initiate their difficult process of psychological and emotional healing—all the while rejuvenating their sense of hope?

Beeling offered a prayer. He introduced it by conceding that "no words" could express the sentiment they shared, yet he would try, on their behalf, to express their thanks and acknowledge their "deep, deep, debt to Almighty God." The captain continued,

> Our Heavenly Father, we see this day as one minute and yet a lifetime for all of us. We thank You for the courage of those who gave their lives in saving their shipmates today. We humbly ask You to grant them peace and to their loved ones the consolation and strength to bear their loss.

Acknowledging the temptation to despair, the CO asked, "Help us to renew the faith we have in you." Resisting the natural tendency toward existentialist anguish in the face of what seems to be a tragic absurdity, Beeling instead turned the occasion toward greater faith:

> May we remember You as You have remembered us today. From our hearts we turn to You now knowing that You have been at our sides at every minute of this day. Heavenly Father, help us to rebuild and re-man our ship so that our brothers who died today may not have made a fruitless sacrifice.

Piety may be broadly understood as the acknowledgment that the leader is not the beginning and end of his own wisdom. Someone has said that nothing great and lasting is accomplished in just one generation. The leader is not morally autonomous in the sense of being his own self-contained moral government; rather, if he is pious, he defers to some conception or combination of Deity, tradition, history, and even colleagues who may possess wisdom greater than his own. The pious leader recognizes that he is answerable—somehow and to someone—for his conduct and his decisions.

LEADERSHIP PRINCIPLES:

- *A leader's greatness is often seen in his acknowledgment that he is answerable to something yet greater than himself, whether that acknowledgment is made to a conception of divinity, a tradition, or even a historical obligation.*
- *Develop a habit of acknowledging that you are not the beginning nor the end of your wisdom and effort.*
- *Today, leading a lifestyle marked by piety may take courage. But the alternative is cowardice.*